Seeing Through the Mind's Eye: Navigating Perspective Taking and Mind Blindness in Autism

Travis Breeding

ISBN: 9798376362747

DEDICATION

THIS BOOK IS DEDICATED TO THE
MANY IDIVIDUALS IN THE WORLD
LIVING WITH ASD AND PEOPLE WHO
LOVE AND SUPPORT THEM. I HOPE
YOU FIND THIS BOOK USEFUL AND
HELPFUL ON YOUR JOURNEY

CONTENTS

ACKNOWLEDGMENTS

I'd to thank my friends and family for always being here
for me and allowing me the time to write. I appreciate all
you do for me.

1 PUTTING ON SOMEONE ELSE'S SHOEES: NAVIGATING THE WORLD OF PERSPECTIVE TAKING IN AUTISM

Introduction:

Perspective taking and mind blindness are important concepts in the field of autism spectrum disorders. These terms refer to an individual's ability to understand and empathize with others' thoughts, feelings, and experiences. This ebook will explore the definitions of perspective taking and mind blindness in the context of autism and provide an overview of their implications for individuals with autism.

Perspective Taking

Perspective taking refers to an individual's ability to understand and imagine the thoughts, feelings, and experiences of others. This skill is essential for social interactions, as it allows individuals to anticipate the responses and behaviors of those around them. It is also a crucial aspect of empathy and moral reasoning.

In individuals with autism, perspective taking can be impaired, leading to difficulties in social interactions and communication. This can result in difficulties in building relationships, reading social cues, and responding appropriately to the emotions and needs of others.

Mind Blindness

Mind blindness, also known as "theory of mind" deficiency, refers to an individual's inability to understand that others have beliefs, desires, and intentions that differ from their own. This concept was first introduced by Simon Baron-Cohen in 1985 and has since been a key aspect of research on autism.

Individuals with mind blindness may have difficulty understanding that others can have different perspectives, beliefs, and intentions. This can lead to difficulties in social interactions, as they may misinterpret the motivations and behaviors of others. It can also impact their ability to form and maintain relationships, as they may not understand the social cues and expectations of others.

Implications for Individuals with Autism

Perspective taking and mind blindness are important considerations for individuals with autism and those who interact with them. Understanding these concepts can help in developing effective strategies for supporting individuals with autism in their daily lives, including social interactions, communication, and relationships.

Additionally, interventions such as social skills training and therapy can help individuals with autism improve their perspective taking and mind blindness abilities. These interventions may include role-playing, video modeling, and other techniques that help individuals learn and practice new social skills.

Conclusion:

In conclusion, perspective taking and mind blindness are critical concepts in the understanding of autism. Impairments in these areas can have significant impacts on the daily lives of individuals with autism and their ability to form and maintain relationships. By increasing our understanding of these concepts, we can better support individuals with autism in their development and daily life experiences.

Introduction:

Autism Spectrum Disorders (ASD) are a group of neurodevelopmental disorders characterized by difficulties in social interaction, communication, and repetitive behaviors or interests. It is estimated that 1 in 59 children in the United States are diagnosed with autism, making it a prevalent and important area of study.

This ebook will provide an overview of autism spectrum disorders, including its symptoms, causes, and treatments. It will also discuss current research and future directions in the field of autism.

Symptoms of Autism Spectrum Disorders

Autism spectrum disorders are characterized by three main areas of difficulty: social interaction, communication, and repetitive behaviors or interests.

Social interaction difficulties may include difficulty forming relationships, reading social cues, and expressing emotions. Communication difficulties may include delayed language development, difficulty with conversational skills, and repetitive use of language. Repetitive behaviors or interests may include repetitive movements, intense interests in specific topics, and strict adherence to routines.

Causes of Autism Spectrum Disorders

The exact causes of autism spectrum disorders are not yet fully understood, but research suggests that a combination of genetic and environmental factors play a role.

Genetic factors may include variations in specific genes that influence brain development. Environmental factors may include prenatal exposure to toxins, maternal infection during pregnancy, and complications during delivery.

Treatments for Autism Spectrum Disorders

There is no cure for autism spectrum disorders, but early and intensive intervention can significantly improve outcomes for individuals with autism.

Treatment options may include behavioral and developmental therapies, medication, and educational interventions. Behavioral therapies, such as Applied Behavior Analysis (ABA), focus on teaching individuals with autism new skills and behaviors. Developmental therapies, such as speech and language therapy, focus on improving communication and social skills.

Current Research and Future Directions

Autism research is an active and rapidly evolving field. Currently, researchers are focused on identifying the underlying causes of autism and developing new and improved treatments.

Future directions in the field of autism may include the use of new technologies, such as brain imaging and genetic sequencing, to better understand the biology of autism. Additionally, researchers are exploring new therapies, such as mind-body interventions, to help individuals with autism manage their symptoms.

Conclusion:

In conclusion, autism spectrum disorders are complex and multifaceted conditions that can have significant impacts on individuals and their families. While there is no cure for autism, early and intensive intervention can greatly improve outcomes. Through continued research and advances in treatment, we can hope for a brighter future for individuals with autism and their families.

Introduction:

Perspective taking and mind blindness are important concepts in the field of autism spectrum disorders. These terms refer to an individual's ability to understand and empathize with others' thoughts, feelings, and experiences, and their relationship to autism is a crucial area of study.

This ebook will explore the relationship between perspective taking and mind blindness in the context of autism, including their definition, causes, and implications.

Definition of Perspective Taking and Mind Blindness

Perspective taking refers to an individual's ability to understand and imagine the thoughts, feelings, and experiences of others. Mind blindness, also known as "theory of mind" deficiency, refers to an individual's inability to understand that others have beliefs, desires, and intentions that differ from their own.

Relationship between Perspective Taking and Mind Blindness in Autism

In individuals with autism, perspective taking and mind blindness are often impaired, leading to difficulties in social interactions and communication. This can result in difficulties in building relationships, reading social cues, and responding appropriately to the emotions and needs of others.

These impairments in perspective taking and mind blindness can also contribute to repetitive behaviors and interests, as individuals with autism may have difficulty understanding the motivations and behaviors of others.

Causes of Impairments in Perspective

Taking and Mind Blindness in Autism

The exact causes of impairments in perspective taking and mind blindness in autism are not yet fully understood, but research suggests that they are related to disruptions in the development of the brain's social cognition network.

Additionally, genetic factors may play a role in the development of impairments in perspective taking and mind blindness in autism. Studies have shown that variations in specific genes are associated with the development of these impairments.

Implications for Individuals with Autism

The impairments in perspective taking and mind blindness in autism can have significant impacts on the daily lives of individuals with autism and their ability to form and maintain relationships.

Understanding these impairments is

important for developing effective
strategies for supporting individuals with
autism in their daily lives, including social
interactions, communication, and
relationships. Additionally, interventions
such as social skills training and therapy can
help individuals with autism improve their
perspective taking and mind blindness
abilities.

Conclusion:

In conclusion, the relationship between
perspective taking and mind blindness in
autism is complex and multifaceted.
Impairments in these areas can have
significant impacts on the daily lives of
individuals with autism and their ability to
form and maintain relationships. By
continuing to research and understand the
relationship between perspective taking
and mind blindness in autism, we can better
support individuals with autism in their
development and daily life experiences.

2 THE POWER OF PERSPECTIVE TAKING

Introduction:

Perspective taking is a crucial aspect of human social interaction and communication, and it is essential for developing and maintaining healthy relationships. This term refers to an individual's ability to understand and empathize with others' thoughts, feelings, and experiences.

This ebook will provide a comprehensive overview of perspective taking, including its definition, development, and applications.

Definition of Perspective Taking

Perspective taking refers to an individual's ability to understand and imagine the thoughts, feelings, and experiences of others. This ability allows individuals to understand the perspectives of others and to respond to their emotions and needs appropriately.

Development of Perspective Taking

Perspective taking abilities develop gradually over time, beginning in early childhood and continuing into adulthood. During childhood, children develop their understanding of others' perspectives through interactions with others, including parents, caregivers, and peers.

Additionally, children learn to understand the perspectives of others through socialization and play, as they learn to take on different roles and understand the motivations of others.

Applications of Perspective Taking

Perspective taking has a wide range of applications in various areas of life, including relationships, education, and the workplace.

In relationships, perspective taking is essential for building trust and empathy, as it allows individuals to understand and respond to the needs and emotions of their partners.

In education, perspective taking is an important component of effective learning, as it allows students to understand the perspectives of their classmates and teachers, and to respond appropriately to their needs and emotions.

In the workplace, perspective taking is essential for effective collaboration and teamwork, as it allows individuals to understand the perspectives of their colleagues and to work together effectively to achieve shared goals.

Importance of Perspective Taking in Society

Perspective taking is a critical aspect of human social interaction and communication, and it is essential for building healthy relationships and promoting social harmony. By understanding the perspectives of others, individuals are able to develop empathy and compassion, and to respond to the needs and emotions of others in a meaningful and appropriate way.

Conclusion:

In conclusion, perspective taking is a complex and multifaceted ability that plays a crucial role in human social interaction and communication. It is essential for building healthy relationships, effective learning, and effective collaboration in the workplace. By continuing to understand and develop our perspective taking abilities, we can promote social harmony and build stronger, more meaningful relationships with those around us.

Introduction:

Perspective taking is a crucial aspect of human social interaction and communication, and it is essential for developing and maintaining healthy relationships. This term refers to an individual's ability to understand and empathize with others' thoughts, feelings, and experiences.

This ebook will provide a comprehensive overview of the process of perspective taking, including its development, applications, and benefits.

Definition of Perspective Taking

Perspective taking refers to an individual's ability to understand and imagine the thoughts, feelings, and experiences of others. This ability allows individuals to understand the perspectives of others and to respond to their emotions and needs appropriately.

Development of Perspective Taking

The development of perspective taking begins in early childhood and continues into adulthood. Children develop their understanding of others' perspectives through interactions with others, including parents, caregivers, and peers. Additionally, children learn to understand the perspectives of others through socialization and play, as they learn to take on different roles and understand the motivations of others.

The Process of Perspective Taking

The process of perspective taking involves several steps, including:

Attention: The first step in perspective taking is to pay attention to others and their emotions and behaviors.

Imagination: The next step is to imagine the thoughts, feelings, and experiences of others. This requires individuals to take on the perspective of others and to understand their motivations and behaviors.

Empathy: The final step in the process of perspective taking is to respond to the emotions and needs of others with empathy and compassion. This involves understanding and responding appropriately to the emotions and needs of others.

Applications of Perspective Taking

Perspective taking has a wide range of applications in various areas of life, including relationships, education, and the workplace.

In relationships, perspective taking is essential for building trust and empathy, as it allows individuals to understand and respond to the needs and emotions of their partners.

In education, perspective taking is an important component of effective learning, as it allows students to understand the perspectives of their classmates and teachers, and to respond appropriately to their needs and emotions.

In the workplace, perspective taking is essential for effective collaboration and teamwork, as it allows individuals to understand the perspectives of their colleagues and to work together effectively to achieve shared goals.

Benefits of Perspective Taking

The benefits of perspective taking are numerous, including:

Improved Relationships: Perspective taking allows individuals to build stronger, more meaningful relationships with those around them.

Increased Empathy: Perspective taking helps individuals to develop empathy and compassion, allowing them to respond appropriately to the emotions and needs of others.

Enhanced Learning: Perspective taking is an important component of effective learning, allowing students to understand the perspectives of their classmates and teachers and to respond appropriately to their needs and emotions.

Effective Collaboration: In the workplace, perspective taking is essential for effective collaboration and teamwork, allowing individuals to understand the perspectives of their colleagues and to work together effectively to achieve shared goals.

Conclusion:

In conclusion, the process of perspective taking is a complex and multifaceted ability that plays a crucial role in human social interaction and communication. It is essential for building healthy relationships, effective learning, and effective collaboration in the workplace. By continuing to understand and develop our perspective taking abilities, we can promote social harmony and build stronger, more meaningful relationships with those around us.

Introduction:

Perspective taking is an essential aspect of human social interaction and communication. It refers to an individual's ability to understand and empathize with others' thoughts, feelings, and experiences. In this ebook, we will examine the development of perspective taking in typically developing individuals.

Definition of Perspective Taking

Perspective taking refers to an individual's ability to understand and imagine the thoughts, feelings, and experiences of others. This ability allows individuals to understand the perspectives of others and to respond to their emotions and needs appropriately.

The Development of Perspective Taking

The development of perspective taking begins in early childhood and continues into adulthood. Children develop their understanding of others' perspectives through interactions with others, including parents, caregivers, and peers. Additionally, children learn to understand the perspectives of others through socialization and play, as they learn to take on different roles and understand the motivations of others.

Early Childhood Development of Perspective Taking

In early childhood, the development of perspective taking is influenced by several factors, including:

Parent-Child Interactions: Children learn to understand the perspectives of others through interactions with their parents and caregivers, who model perspective taking and help children to develop empathy and compassion.

Play: Play is an important factor in the development of perspective taking, as children learn to take on different roles and understand the motivations of others.

Theory of Mind: Children develop their understanding of others' perspectives through their developing theory of mind, which refers to their ability to understand that others have thoughts, feelings, and experiences that are different from their own.

Adolescent and Adult Development of Perspective Taking

As individuals enter adolescence and adulthood, their perspective taking abilities continue to develop and mature. Adolescents and adults develop their understanding of others' perspectives through experiences, including relationships, education, and the workplace.

In relationships, perspective taking is essential for building trust and empathy, as it allows individuals to understand and respond to the needs and emotions of their partners.

In education, perspective taking is an important component of effective learning, as it allows students to understand the perspectives of their classmates and teachers, and to respond appropriately to their needs and emotions.

In the workplace, perspective taking is essential for effective collaboration and teamwork, as it allows individuals to understand the perspectives of their colleagues and to work together effectively to achieve shared goals.

Factors That Influence the Development of Perspective Taking

The development of perspective taking is influenced by several factors, including:

Family Environment: Family environment, including parent-child interactions and family relationships, plays a significant role in the development of perspective taking.

Socialization: Socialization, including experiences with peers and community involvement, also plays a role in the development of perspective taking.

Education: Education and exposure to diverse perspectives and experiences can also enhance perspective taking abilities.

Personal Traits: Personal traits, such as empathy and compassion, also play a role in the development of perspective taking.

Conclusion:

In conclusion, the development of perspective taking is a complex and multifaceted process that begins in early childhood and continues into adulthood. It is influenced by a variety of factors, including parent-child interactions, play, education, and personal traits. By understanding the development of perspective taking, we can better understand the importance of this ability in human social interaction and communication and can work to enhance our own perspective taking abilities.

Introduction:

Autism Spectrum Disorders (ASD) are a group of developmental disorders characterized by difficulties in social interaction, communication, and behavior. One of the core challenges faced by individuals with autism is difficulty in perspective taking, which refers to the ability to understand and empathize with others' thoughts, feelings, and experiences. In this ebook, we will examine the challenges with perspective taking in individuals with autism spectrum disorders.

Definition of Autism Spectrum Disorders

Autism Spectrum Disorders are a group of developmental disorders that affect an individual's ability to communicate and interact with others. They are characterized by difficulties in social interaction, communication, and behavior. Individuals with autism may also experience sensory sensitivities and repetitive behaviors.

The Importance of Perspective Taking in Autism Spectrum Disorders

Perspective taking is an essential aspect of human social interaction and communication. It allows individuals to understand the perspectives of others and respond to their emotions and needs appropriately. For individuals with autism, perspective taking can be a significant challenge, leading to difficulties in building relationships, participating in group activities, and understanding the emotions and needs of others.

The Challenges with Perspective Taking in Individuals with Autism Spectrum Disorders

Theory of Mind: Individuals with autism may have difficulty understanding that others have thoughts, feelings, and experiences that are different from their own. This difficulty is referred to as a "theory of mind" deficit and is a significant challenge for individuals with autism in understanding and empathizing with the perspectives of others.

Empathy: Individuals with autism may also have difficulty experiencing empathy for others, which can impact their ability to understand and respond appropriately to the emotions and needs of others.

Social Interactions: Difficulty with perspective taking can also impact social interactions, leading to difficulties in building relationships, participating in group activities, and understanding the perspectives of others in social situations.

Sensory Sensitivities: Some individuals with autism may experience sensory sensitivities, which can impact their ability to understand the perspectives of others and respond appropriately to their emotions and needs.

Strategies for Enhancing Perspective Taking in Individuals with Autism Spectrum Disorders

While perspective taking can be a significant challenge for individuals with autism, there are strategies that can be used to enhance their ability to understand and empathize with the perspectives of others. These strategies include:

Social Skills Training: Social skills training can help individuals with autism to develop the skills necessary for effective social interaction, including perspective taking.

Empathy Training: Empathy training can help individuals with autism to develop their ability to experience empathy for others and to understand and respond appropriately to their emotions and needs.

Play-Based Interventions: Play-based

interventions can be an effective way to develop perspective taking abilities in children with autism. These interventions can include role-play activities and games that help children to understand the perspectives of others and to develop empathy and compassion.

Sensory Integration Therapy: Sensory integration therapy can help individuals with autism to manage their sensory sensitivities, which can impact their ability to understand and empathize with the perspectives of others.

Conclusion

In conclusion, perspective taking can be a significant challenge for individuals with autism spectrum disorders. However, with the right support and strategies, individuals with autism can develop their ability to understand and empathize with the perspectives of others. By enhancing perspective taking abilities, individuals with autism can improve their social interactions, build meaningful relationships, and participate in group activities with greater success.

3 MIND BLINDNESS

Introduction

Mind blindness is a term used to describe one of the core challenges faced by individuals with autism spectrum disorders. This term refers to the difficulty that individuals with autism have in understanding the mental states and perspectives of others. In this ebook, we will examine the definition of mind blindness and its implications for individuals with autism.

Definition of Autism Spectrum Disorders

Autism Spectrum Disorders (ASD) are a group of developmental disorders characterized by difficulties in social interaction, communication, and behavior. Individuals with autism may also experience sensory sensitivities and repetitive behaviors.

Definition of Mind Blindness

Mind blindness refers to the difficulty that individuals with autism have in understanding the mental states and perspectives of others. This term was first introduced by Simon Baron-Cohen and his colleagues and refers to the inability to recognize and understand that other people have their own thoughts, feelings, and experiences.

The Implications of Mind Blindness in Autism Spectrum Disorders

Difficulty with Perspective Taking: Mind blindness can lead to difficulties in perspective taking, which is the ability to understand and empathize with the thoughts, feelings, and experiences of others.

Challenges in Social Interactions: Individuals with mind blindness may have difficulty participating in social interactions and building relationships with others.

Difficulty Understanding Emotions: Individuals with mind blindness may have difficulty recognizing and understanding the emotions of others, which can impact their ability to respond appropriately.

Sensory Sensitivities: Some individuals with autism may experience sensory sensitivities, which can further impact their ability to understand the mental states and perspectives of others.

Strategies for Overcoming Mind Blindness in Individuals with Autism Spectrum Disorders

While mind blindness can be a significant challenge for individuals with autism, there are strategies that can be used to enhance their ability to understand the mental states and perspectives of others. These strategies include:

Social Skills Training: Social skills training can help individuals with autism to develop the skills necessary for effective social interaction, including perspective taking.

Empathy Training: Empathy training can help individuals with autism to develop their ability to experience empathy for others and to understand and respond appropriately to their emotions and needs.

Play-Based Interventions: Play-based interventions can be an effective way to develop perspective taking abilities in children with autism. These interventions can include role-play activities and games that help children to understand the perspectives of others and to develop empathy and compassion.

Sensory Integration Therapy: Sensory integration therapy can help individuals with autism to manage their sensory sensitivities, which can impact their ability to understand and empathize with the perspectives of others.

Conclusion

In conclusion, mind blindness is a significant challenge faced by individuals with autism spectrum disorders. However, with the right support and strategies, individuals with autism can overcome this challenge and develop their ability to understand the mental states and perspectives of others. By enhancing their perspective taking abilities, individuals with autism can improve their social interactions, build meaningful relationships, and participate in group activities with greater success.

Introduction:

Mind-blindness, also known as "theory of mind" deficiency, is a concept in psychology that refers to the inability of individuals to understand the thoughts, beliefs, and emotions of others. This can lead to difficulties in social interactions, communication, and empathy.

What is Mind-Blindness?

In this chapter, we will define mind-blindness and explore its symptoms and causes. Mind-blindness is a cognitive impairment that affects a person's ability to understand the mental states of others. This can result in difficulties in recognizing and interpreting social cues, making decisions, and forming relationships.

Causes of Mind-Blindness

In this chapter, we will explore the

underlying causes of mind-blindness. Some of the most common causes include neurological or developmental disorders such as autism, Asperger's syndrome, and schizophrenia. Other potential causes include brain injuries, genetic predisposition, and environmental factors such as stress or trauma.

Symptoms of Mind-Blindness

In this chapter, we will describe the symptoms of mind-blindness. These can include difficulty in understanding sarcasm, recognizing emotions in others, and interpreting social cues. Other symptoms may include difficulty in making and maintaining social connections, lack of empathy, and poor communication skills.

Diagnosing Mind-Blindness

In this chapter, we will discuss the process of diagnosing mind-blindness. A professional evaluation, including a medical

and psychological evaluation, may be
necessary to determine if a person has
mind-blindness. This evaluation may include
a review of the individual's medical history,
observation of social interactions, and the
administration of standardized tests.

Treating Mind-Blindness

In this chapter, we will explore the different
treatment options available for mind-
blindness. These may include therapy,
medication, and educational interventions.
Therapy can help individuals develop the
skills they need to understand the thoughts,
beliefs, and emotions of others, while
medication can help manage the symptoms
of mind-blindness. Educational
interventions can help individuals learn new
skills and improve their ability to function in
social situations.

Conclusion:

In conclusion, mind-blindness is a complex

condition that can have a profound impact on an individual's life. Understanding the causes, symptoms, and treatment options can help those affected by mind-blindness to lead fulfilling and productive lives. With the right support and resources, individuals with mind-blindness can overcome this challenge and achieve their full potential.

Introduction:

Mind-blindness, also known as "theory of mind" deficiency, is a concept in psychology that refers to the inability of individuals to understand the thoughts, beliefs, and emotions of others. This ability typically develops over time in typically developing individuals and plays a crucial role in social interaction and communication.

What is Mind-Blindness?

In this chapter, we will define mind-blindness and explore its significance in social and emotional development. Mind-blindness refers to the inability to understand the mental states of others, including their thoughts, beliefs, and emotions. It is a crucial component of social and emotional development, as it allows individuals to understand the motivations and behaviors of others and to respond appropriately.

The Development of Mind-Blindness in Typically Developing Individuals

In this chapter, we will explore the development of mind-blindness in typically developing individuals. Research has shown that this ability typically develops in stages, starting in early childhood and continuing through adolescence and into adulthood. The development of mind-blindness is influenced by a variety of factors, including social experiences, language development, and cognitive development.

The Role of Social Experiences in the Development of Mind-Blindness

In this chapter, we will explore the role of social experiences in the development of mind-blindness. Research has shown that social experiences play a crucial role in the development of this ability. For example, early social interactions with parents and peers can help children learn to understand the thoughts and feelings of others.

The Role of Language in the Development of Mind-Blindness

In this chapter, we will explore the role of language in the development of mind-blindness. Research has shown that language plays a crucial role in the development of this ability, as it provides children with the tools they need to understand and express their own thoughts and emotions, as well as those of others.

The Role of Cognitive Development in the

Development of Mind-Blindness

In this chapter, we will explore the role of cognitive development in the development of mind-blindness. Research has shown that cognitive development, including the development of executive functioning and theory of mind, plays a crucial role in the development of this ability. As children grow and their cognitive abilities mature, they become better equipped to understand the mental states of others.

Conclusion:

In conclusion, the development of mind-blindness is a complex process that unfolds over time in typically developing individuals. This ability plays a crucial role in social and emotional development, allowing individuals to understand the thoughts, beliefs, and emotions of others. The development of mind-blindness is influenced by a variety of factors, including social experiences, language development, and cognitive development. By understanding these factors, we can gain a better understanding of this important aspect of human development.

Introduction:

Autism Spectrum Disorders (ASD) are a group of developmental disorders that can cause significant challenges in social interaction and communication. One of the key features of autism is mind-blindness, also known as "theory of mind" deficiency, which refers to the inability to understand the thoughts, beliefs, and emotions of others. This can lead to significant difficulties in social interaction and communication.

What is Mind-Blindness?

In this chapter, we will define mind-blindness and explore its significance in individuals with autism. Mind-blindness refers to the inability to understand the mental states of others, including their thoughts, beliefs, and emotions. This can lead to significant difficulties in social interaction and communication, particularly for individuals with autism.

The Prevalence of Mind-Blindness in Individuals with Autism

In this chapter, we will explore the prevalence of mind-blindness in individuals with autism. Research has shown that mind-blindness is a common feature of autism and can cause significant difficulties in social interaction and communication. In some cases, mind-blindness can be so severe that it affects an individual's ability to form and maintain relationships.

The Challenges of Mind-Blindness in Individuals with Autism

In this chapter, we will explore the challenges posed by mind-blindness in individuals with autism. These challenges can include difficulty in recognizing and interpreting social cues, making decisions, and forming relationships. In some cases, mind-blindness can also lead to difficulties in communication, including an inability to understand sarcasm, irony, and other forms of nonverbal communication.

Strategies for Overcoming Mind-Blindness in Individuals with Autism

In this chapter, we will discuss strategies for overcoming mind-blindness in individuals with autism. These strategies may include therapy, educational interventions, and the use of assistive technology. Therapy can help individuals develop the skills they need to understand the thoughts, beliefs, and emotions of others, while educational interventions can help individuals learn new skills and improve their ability to function in social situations. Assistive technology, such as social skills training software, can also be helpful in overcoming mind-blindness.

Supporting Individuals with Autism and Mind-Blindness

In this chapter, we will discuss ways to support individuals with autism and mind-blindness. This may include providing education and resources for family members, promoting social skills training and therapy, and advocating for the needs of individuals with autism. In addition, it is important to provide a supportive and inclusive environment that helps individuals with autism feel valued and accepted.

Conclusion:

In conclusion, mind-blindness can pose significant challenges for individuals with autism. However, with the right support and resources, individuals with autism and mind-blindness can overcome this challenge and lead fulfilling and productive lives. By understanding the challenges posed by mind-blindness and exploring strategies for overcoming these challenges, we can help individuals with autism reach their full potential.

4 THEORIES OF PERSPECTIVE TAKING AND MIND BLINDNESS

Introduction:

Theory of mind (ToM) is an important concept in the field of psychology that refers to the ability to understand the thoughts, feelings, and beliefs of others. This ability is critical for effective communication and social interaction, and is considered a key component of human intelligence.

Defining Theory of Mind

In this chapter, we will define theory of mind and explore its significance in human development. Theory of mind refers to the ability to understand that other people have their own thoughts, feelings, and beliefs that are different from one's own. This ability is essential for effective communication and social interaction, and is considered a key component of human intelligence.

The Development of Theory of Mind

In this chapter, we will explore the development of theory of mind in children. Research has shown that the ability to understand the thoughts, feelings, and beliefs of others develops gradually over time, and is influenced by a variety of factors including experience, social interaction, and genetics.

The Importance of Theory of Mind in Social Interaction

In this chapter, we will discuss the importance of theory of mind in social interaction. The ability to understand the thoughts, feelings, and beliefs of others is critical for effective communication and social interaction, and is essential for building and maintaining relationships.

Challenges with Theory of Mind

In this chapter, we will explore the challenges that can arise when theory of mind is impaired. Some individuals, such as those with autism or schizophrenia, may have difficulty understanding the thoughts, feelings, and beliefs of others. This can lead to significant difficulties in communication and social interaction.

Strategies for Improving Theory of Mind

In this chapter, we will discuss strategies for improving theory of mind. These strategies may include therapy, educational interventions, and the use of assistive technology. Therapy can help individuals develop the skills they need to understand the thoughts, feelings, and beliefs of others, while educational interventions can help individuals learn new skills and improve their ability to function in social situations. Assistive technology, such as social skills training software, can also be helpful in improving theory of mind.

The Role of Culture and Society in Theory of Mind

In this chapter, we will discuss the role that culture and society play in shaping theory of mind. Research has shown that culture and societal norms can influence the development of theory of mind and shape the way in which individuals understand the thoughts, feelings, and beliefs of others.

Conclusion:

In conclusion, theory of mind is a critical aspect of human intelligence and plays a crucial role in effective communication and social interaction. By understanding the development of theory of mind and exploring strategies for improving this ability, we can help individuals reach their full potential and lead fulfilling and productive lives.

Introduction:

Simulation theory is a philosophical and psychological concept that suggests that human cognition is based on the simulation of experiences in the mind, rather than the direct processing of external stimuli. This theory has been widely discussed in the fields of philosophy, psychology, and cognitive science, and has important implications for our understanding of human perception, thought, and action.

Defining Simulation Theory

In this chapter, we will define simulation theory and explore its central tenets. Simulation theory proposes that human cognition is based on the simulation of experiences in the mind, rather than the direct processing of external stimuli. This means that when we think about or experience something, we are running a mental simulation of that experience, rather than directly perceiving the world around us.

The History of Simulation Theory

In this chapter, we will explore the history of simulation theory, from its roots in ancient philosophy to its current status as a widely accepted concept in cognitive science. We will examine the work of early philosophers such as Plato and Descartes, and trace the development of simulation theory through the 20th century, highlighting key developments and debates along the way.

The Evidence for Simulation Theory

In this chapter, we will examine the evidence for simulation theory. We will explore the findings of empirical studies, including brain imaging and behavioral experiments, that have provided support for the idea that human cognition is based on the simulation of experiences in the mind. We will also examine the challenges to simulation theory and the alternative explanations that have been put forward.

The Implications of Simulation Theory

In this chapter, we will discuss the implications of simulation theory for our understanding of human perception, thought, and action. We will explore how simulation theory affects our understanding of the nature of reality, the role of

imagination in thought, and the
mechanisms underlying human decision-
making.

Simulation Theory and Artificial Intelligence

In this chapter, we will discuss the
implications of simulation theory for the
field of artificial intelligence. We will
explore how simulation theory informs the
development of artificial systems that can
perceive, think, and act like humans, and
examine the challenges and limitations of
this endeavor.

The Future of Simulation Theory

In this chapter, we will discuss the future of
simulation theory and the directions in
which the field is likely to move. We will
examine the challenges facing simulation
theory, including the need for more
empirical evidence and the need to
incorporate new findings from other fields,

such as neuroscience and philosophy. We will also examine the potential benefits of simulation theory, including the development of new technologies and the advancement of our understanding of human cognition.

Conclusion:

In conclusion, simulation theory is a fascinating and important concept that has far-reaching implications for our understanding of human cognition. By exploring the history, evidence, and implications of simulation theory, we can gain a deeper understanding of the mechanisms underlying human perception, thought, and action, and the potential for developing artificial systems that can simulate human experience.

Introduction:

Weak Central Coherence (WCC) theory is a cognitive model that proposes that individuals with autism spectrum disorders (ASD) have difficulties integrating information from different sources and tend to focus on specific details rather than on the overall context or situation. This theory provides important insights into the cognitive processes that underlie the behaviors and experiences of individuals with autism.

Defining Weak Central Coherence Theory

In this chapter, we will define Weak Central Coherence theory and explore its central tenets. We will examine the key components of WCC, including the focus on details and difficulties in integrating information, and the ways in which these characteristics are thought to impact the perception and interpretation of the world in individuals with autism.

The History of Weak Central Coherence Theory

In this chapter, we will explore the history of Weak Central Coherence theory, from its earliest origins to its current status as a widely accepted cognitive model in the field of autism research. We will examine the key developments and debates that have shaped the evolution of WCC theory, and discuss the ways in which this theory has informed our understanding of autism and related conditions.

Evidence for Weak Central Coherence Theory

In this chapter, we will examine the evidence for Weak Central Coherence theory. We will explore the findings of empirical studies, including brain imaging, behavioral experiments, and studies of individual experiences, that have provided support for the idea that individuals with autism tend to focus on specific details and have difficulties integrating information. We will also examine the challenges to WCC theory and the alternative explanations that have been put forward.

The Implications of Weak Central Coherence Theory

In this chapter, we will discuss the implications of Weak Central Coherence theory for our understanding of autism and related conditions. We will explore how WCC theory informs our understanding of the cognitive and neural processes that underlie the behaviors and experiences of individuals with autism, and examine the ways in which this knowledge can be used to improve diagnosis and treatment.

Weak Central Coherence Theory and Interventions

In this chapter, we will discuss the implications of Weak Central Coherence theory for the development of interventions for individuals with autism. We will explore the ways in which WCC theory can inform the design and implementation of therapeutic interventions, including behavioral and educational approaches, and examine the evidence for the effectiveness of these interventions.

The Future of Weak Central Coherence Theory

In this chapter, we will discuss the future of Weak Central Coherence theory and the directions in which the field is likely to move. We will examine the challenges facing WCC theory, including the need for more empirical evidence and the need to incorporate new findings from other fields, such as neuroscience and psychology. We will also examine the potential benefits of WCC theory, including the development of new interventions and the advancement of our understanding of autism and related conditions.

Conclusion:

In conclusion, Weak Central Coherence theory is a crucial and groundbreaking cognitive model that has important implications for our understanding of autism and related conditions. By exploring the history, evidence, and implications of WCC theory, we can gain a deeper understanding of the cognitive processes that underlie the behaviors and experiences of individuals with autism, and the potential for improving diagnosis and treatment.

Introduction:

Executive functioning (EF) refers to the cognitive processes responsible for goal-directed behavior, planning, problem-solving, and decision-making. Executive functioning theory seeks to understand the underlying mechanisms of these processes and how they interact with other cognitive and neural systems. This theory has important implications for our understanding of a wide range of conditions, including autism spectrum disorders, attention deficit hyperactivity disorder, and traumatic brain injury.

Defining Executive Functioning Theory

In this chapter, we will define executive functioning and explore its central tenets. We will examine the key components of EF, including working memory, inhibitory control, and cognitive flexibility, and discuss how these processes interact to support goal-directed behavior and decision-making.

The History of Executive Functioning Theory

In this chapter, we will explore the history

of executive functioning theory, from its earliest origins to its current status as a widely accepted cognitive model in the field of neuroscience and psychology. We will examine the key developments and debates that have shaped the evolution of EF theory, and discuss the ways in which this theory has informed our understanding of a wide range of conditions and behaviors.

Evidence for Executive Functioning Theory

In this chapter, we will examine the evidence for executive functioning theory. We will explore the findings of empirical studies, including brain imaging, behavioral experiments, and studies of individual experiences, that have provided support for the idea that EF is a distinct and important cognitive process. We will also examine the challenges to EF theory and the alternative explanations that have been put forward.

The Implications of Executive Functioning

Theory

In this chapter, we will discuss the implications of executive functioning theory for our understanding of a wide range of conditions, including autism spectrum disorders, attention deficit hyperactivity disorder, and traumatic brain injury. We will explore how EF theory informs our understanding of the cognitive and neural processes that underlie these conditions, and examine the ways in which this knowledge can be used to improve diagnosis and treatment.

Executive Functioning Theory and Interventions

In this chapter, we will discuss the implications of executive functioning theory for the development of interventions for individuals with conditions that affect EF. We will explore the ways in which EF theory can inform the design and implementation of therapeutic interventions, including behavioral and educational approaches, and examine the evidence for the effectiveness of these interventions.

The Future of Executive Functioning Theory

In this chapter, we will discuss the future of executive functioning theory and the directions in which the field is likely to move. We will examine the challenges facing EF theory, including the need for more empirical evidence and the need to incorporate new findings from other fields, such as neuroscience and psychology. We will also examine the potential benefits of EF theory, including the development of new interventions and the advancement of our understanding of conditions that affect EF.

Conclusion:

In conclusion, executive functioning theory

is a crucial and groundbreaking cognitive model that has important implications for our understanding of a wide range of conditions and behaviors. By exploring the history, evidence, and implications of EF theory, we can gain a deeper understanding of the cognitive processes that underlie goal-directed behavior, planning, problem-solving, and decision-making, and the potential for improving diagnosis and treatment.

5 DIAGNOSIS OF AUTISM SPECTRUM DISORDER

Introduction:

Autism Spectrum Disorder (ASD) is a complex developmental disorder that affects communication, social interaction, and behavior. In recent years, autism has become a widely recognized and studied condition, with significant advances made in our understanding of its causes, symptoms, and treatments. Despite this progress, there is still much that remains unknown about autism, and the condition remains a source of confusion and misinformation for many people.

Defining Autism Spectrum Disorder

In this chapter, we will provide a comprehensive definition of autism spectrum disorder. We will explore the key features and symptoms of autism, including difficulties with communication, social interaction, and repetitive behaviors, and examine the ways in which these symptoms are diagnosed and classified.

The History of Autism Spectrum Disorder

In this chapter, we will explore the history of autism spectrum disorder, from its earliest descriptions in the 1940s to its current status as a widely recognized and studied condition. We will examine the key developments and debates that have shaped our understanding of autism, and discuss the ways in which this understanding has evolved over time.

Causes and Risk Factors of Autism Spectrum Disorder

In this chapter, we will examine the causes and risk factors of autism spectrum disorder. We will explore the role of genetics, the environment, and brain development in the development of autism, and discuss the ways in which these factors interact to produce the symptoms of the condition.

Symptoms of Autism Spectrum Disorder

In this chapter, we will examine the symptoms of autism spectrum disorder in greater detail. We will explore the key features of autism, including difficulties with communication, social interaction, and repetitive behaviors, and discuss the ways in which these symptoms vary in intensity and presentation across the autism spectrum.

Diagnosing Autism Spectrum Disorder

In this chapter, we will discuss the process of diagnosing autism spectrum disorder. We will examine the criteria used to diagnose autism, including the Diagnostic and Statistical Manual of Mental Disorders (DSM-5), and explore the role of assessments, including developmental evaluations, behavioral observations, and neuropsychological testing, in the diagnostic process.

Treating and Managing Autism Spectrum Disorder

In this chapter, we will discuss the treatment and management of autism spectrum disorder. We will examine the various therapeutic approaches, including behavioral and educational interventions, pharmacological treatments, and complementary therapies, and explore the evidence for their effectiveness. We will also discuss the role of support and resources, including early intervention programs, advocacy organizations, and support groups, in helping individuals with autism and their families manage the condition.

Living with Autism Spectrum Disorder

In this chapter, we will explore the challenges and opportunities of living with autism spectrum disorder. We will discuss the ways in which individuals with autism and their families can manage the condition, including strategies for coping with symptoms, building relationships, and navigating the educational and employment systems. We will also examine the role of the broader community in promoting understanding and acceptance of autism.

Conclusion:

In conclusion, autism spectrum disorder is a complex and multifaceted condition that affects individuals in a variety of ways. Despite the progress made in our understanding of autism, there is still much that remains unknown about the condition. However, by exploring the definition, history, causes, symptoms, diagnosis, treatment, and management of autism, we can gain a deeper understanding of this condition and the ways in which it affects individuals and their families.

Introduction:

Autism Spectrum Disorder (ASD) is a complex developmental disorder that affects communication, social interaction, and behavior. In recent years, significant advances have been made in our understanding of autism and its diagnosis, with the creation of standardized diagnostic criteria and tools that help healthcare professionals make an accurate diagnosis.

The Diagnostic Process

In this chapter, we will discuss the diagnostic process for autism spectrum disorder. We will examine the role of healthcare professionals, including pediatricians, psychologists, and developmental specialists, in the diagnosis of autism, and explore the importance of early diagnosis and intervention. We will also discuss the key components of the diagnostic process, including developmental evaluations, behavioral observations, and neuropsychological testing.

The Diagnostic Criteria

In this chapter, we will examine the diagnostic criteria for autism spectrum disorder. We will explore the criteria outlined in the Diagnostic and Statistical Manual of Mental Disorders (DSM-5), including the domains of communication, social interaction, and repetitive behaviors and interests, and discuss how these criteria are used to make a diagnosis of autism.

Communication Deficits

In this chapter, we will examine the communication deficits associated with autism spectrum disorder. We will explore the ways in which individuals with autism may struggle with language development, including difficulties with speech and understanding, and discuss the impact these difficulties can have on social interaction and behavior.

Social Interaction Deficits

In this chapter, we will examine the social interaction deficits associated with autism spectrum disorder. We will explore the ways in which individuals with autism may struggle to form and maintain relationships, including difficulties with social cues, nonverbal communication, and empathy, and discuss the impact these difficulties can have on behavior and overall functioning.

Repetitive Behaviors and Interests

In this chapter, we will examine the repetitive behaviors and interests associated with autism spectrum disorder. We will explore the ways in which individuals with autism may engage in repetitive actions, including hand flapping, rocking, and lining up objects, and discuss the role these behaviors may play in the development of more specialized interests, such as an intense focus on a particular topic or object.

The Impact of Severity

In this chapter, we will examine the impact of severity on the diagnosis of autism spectrum disorder. We will explore the ways in which autism symptoms can vary in intensity and presentation across the autism spectrum, and discuss the role of severity in determining the most appropriate treatment and support.

Conclusion:

In conclusion, the criteria for a diagnosis of autism spectrum disorder play a critical role in ensuring that individuals receive an accurate and timely diagnosis and access to appropriate treatment and support. By exploring the diagnostic criteria and the domains of communication, social interaction, and repetitive behaviors and interests, we can gain a deeper understanding of the condition and the ways in which it affects individuals and their families.

Autism Spectrum Disorder (ASD) is a complex developmental disorder that affects communication, social interaction, and behavior. Accurate and timely diagnosis of autism is essential for ensuring that individuals receive the appropriate treatment and support they need. This requires the use of effective and reliable assessment tools.

Screening Tools

In this chapter, we will examine the role of screening tools in the assessment of autism spectrum disorder. We will discuss the different types of screening tools available, including questionnaires, developmental assessments, and behavioral observations, and explore their advantages and limitations.

Diagnostic Tools

In this chapter, we will examine the role of diagnostic tools in the assessment of autism spectrum disorder. We will discuss the different types of diagnostic tools available, including standardized diagnostic assessments, developmental evaluations, and neuropsychological testing, and explore their advantages and limitations.

The Autism Diagnostic Observation Schedule (ADOS)

In this chapter, we will focus on the Autism Diagnostic Observation Schedule (ADOS), a widely used diagnostic tool for the assessment of autism. We will discuss the purpose of the ADOS, its components, and the role it plays in the diagnostic process.

The Diagnostic and Statistical Manual of Mental Disorders (DSM-5)

In this chapter, we will examine the role of the Diagnostic and Statistical Manual of Mental Disorders (DSM-5) in the assessment of autism spectrum disorder. We will discuss the diagnostic criteria for autism outlined in the DSM-5, and explore the ways in which the DSM-5 is used in the diagnostic process.

Interdisciplinary Assessment Teams

In this chapter, we will examine the role of interdisciplinary assessment teams in the assessment of autism spectrum disorder. We will discuss the advantages of working with a team of healthcare professionals, including pediatricians, psychologists, and developmental specialists, and explore the ways in which interdisciplinary teams can collaborate to make an accurate diagnosis.

The Importance of Early Assessment

In this chapter, we will examine the importance of early assessment for autism spectrum disorder. We will discuss the benefits of early diagnosis, including the ability to provide early intervention and support, and explore the ways in which early assessment can impact outcomes and overall functioning.

Conclusion:

In conclusion, assessment tools play a critical role in the diagnosis of autism spectrum disorder. By examining the various screening and diagnostic tools available, including the Autism Diagnostic Observation Schedule (ADOS) and the

Diagnostic and Statistical Manual of Mental Disorders (DSM-5), we can gain a deeper understanding of the importance of accurate and timely diagnosis and the role of effective assessment tools in ensuring that individuals receive the support they need.

Challenges in Diagnosing Autism Spectrum Disorder

Diagnosing Autism Spectrum Disorder (ASD) can be a challenging and complex process. Despite the availability of various assessment tools, there are several factors that can make the diagnosis of autism difficult, including:

Lack of Awareness: There is often a lack of awareness about autism, which can lead to a delay in diagnosis. This can occur because many individuals and their families are not aware of the signs and symptoms of autism, and may not seek a diagnosis.

Misconceptions: There are many misconceptions about autism, which can lead to misunderstandings and misdiagnosis. For example, some individuals may believe that autism only affects young children, or that it is caused by poor parenting.

Varying Symptoms: The symptoms of autism can vary greatly from one individual to another. This can make it difficult for healthcare professionals to diagnose autism, as individuals may not present with the classic signs and symptoms.

Overlapping Symptoms: The symptoms of autism can overlap with other developmental disorders, such as ADHD, making it difficult to make an accurate diagnosis.

Limited Access to Services: Access to diagnostic services can be limited,

particularly in underserved communities.
This can make it difficult for individuals to
receive a diagnosis and receive appropriate
treatment and support.

Inaccurate Diagnostic Tools: Despite the
availability of various assessment tools,
there is no single diagnostic test for autism.
The accuracy of these tools can be limited
by a number of factors, including cultural
and linguistic differences, as well as the
variability of symptoms in individuals with
autism.

Age of Diagnosis: Many individuals with
autism are not diagnosed until later in
childhood, which can result in a delay in
treatment and support. This can be due to a
lack of early screening and recognition of
the signs and symptoms of autism, as well
as a lack of access to diagnostic services.

In conclusion, the diagnosis of autism can
be a challenging and complex process, but

with the right resources, support, and understanding, it is possible to make an accurate diagnosis and provide individuals with the treatment and support they need.

6 OVERVIEW OF INTERVENTIONS FOR IMPROVING PERSPECTIVE TAKING AND MIND BLINDNESS IN AUTISM SPECTRUM DISORDER

Interventions for Improving Perspective Taking and Mind-Blindness in Autism Spectrum Disorders

Autism Spectrum Disorders (ASD) are complex developmental disorders that are characterized by difficulties with social interaction, communication, and repetitive behaviors. One of the core features of autism is mind-blindness, or the difficulty in understanding others' thoughts, feelings, and beliefs. This difficulty in perspective taking can result in significant challenges in social interactions, relationships, and communication. In this chapter, we will provide an overview of interventions that can be used to improve perspective taking and mind-blindness in individuals with autism.

Interventions for Improving Perspective Taking:

Social Stories: Social stories are short narratives that describe social situations and the expected behaviors and responses. They can be used to help individuals with autism understand social cues and perspective taking by providing clear and concrete examples. Social stories can be created specifically for the individual and can be used to address specific challenges and situations.

Video Modeling: Video modeling is a

technique that involves showing individuals with autism a video of someone demonstrating a desired behavior or skill. This can help individuals with autism learn about social cues and perspective taking by seeing it modeled in a real-life scenario.

Role-Playing: Role-playing is a technique that involves practicing social interactions in a safe and controlled environment. Individuals with autism can learn about perspective taking by participating in role-plays that simulate real-life social situations. Role-plays can be used to address specific challenges and help individuals practice and improve their social skills.

Peer-Mediated Interventions: Peer-mediated interventions involve working with typically developing peers to improve social interaction and perspective taking in individuals with autism. This can be done through activities such as cooperative play or social skills groups where individuals with autism can practice their social skills and learn from their peers.

Interventions for Improving Mind-Blindness:

Theory of Mind Training: Theory of mind training is a type of intervention that focuses on teaching individuals with autism about the thoughts, feelings, and beliefs of others. This can be done through various activities, such as comic strip conversations, where individuals are asked to interpret the thoughts and feelings of characters in a comic strip.

Mentalizing Exercises: Mentalizing exercises involve teaching individuals with autism to focus on the mental states of others and consider their thoughts, feelings, and beliefs. These exercises can involve activities such as role-playing and storytelling, where individuals are encouraged to consider the perspectives of others.

Mindfulness Training: Mindfulness training is a type of intervention that involves teaching individuals with autism to be more aware of their thoughts, feelings, and emotions, as well as the thoughts, feelings, and emotions of others. Mindfulness training can help individuals with autism improve their perspective taking by teaching them to be more aware of the emotional and mental states of others.

Social Neuroscience Approaches: Social neuroscience approaches are interventions that involve using neuroimaging and other brain imaging techniques to better understand the neural basis of social cognition in individuals with autism. This information can be used to develop more targeted and effective interventions for improving perspective taking and mind-blindness in individuals with autism.

Conclusion: In conclusion, there are various interventions that can be used to improve perspective taking and mind-blindness in individuals with autism. These interventions can be tailored to the specific needs and abilities of each individual and can help improve their social skills, communication, and relationships. However, it is important to note that the best approach will depend on the individual and their specific needs and abilities. It is recommended that individuals with autism work with a team of professionals, including psychologists, speech therapists, and occupational therapists, to gain perspective taking skills.

Behavioral Interventions for Perspective Taking and Mind-Blindness in Autism Spectrum Disorders

Autism Spectrum Disorders (ASD) are developmental disorders characterized by difficulties in social interaction, communication, and repetitive behaviors. One of the core features of autism is mind-blindness, or the difficulty in understanding others' thoughts, feelings, and beliefs. This difficulty in perspective taking can result in significant challenges in social interactions, relationships, and communication. In this chapter, we will focus on behavioral interventions that can be used to improve perspective taking and mind-blindness in individuals with autism.

Behavioral Interventions for Improving Perspective Taking:

Social Skills Training: Social skills training is a type of behavioral intervention that focuses on teaching individuals with autism the social skills they need to succeed in their daily lives. This can include teaching individuals about social cues, appropriate social behaviors, and perspective taking. Social skills training can be done in individual or group settings and can involve role-playing, video modeling, and other interactive activities.

Contingency Management: Contingency management is a type of behavioral intervention that involves using rewards and consequences to reinforce desired behaviors. In the context of improving perspective taking and mind-blindness, contingency management can be used to reinforce behaviors such as making eye contact, using appropriate social gestures, and considering the perspectives of others.

Cognitive Behavioral Therapy (CBT): CBT is a type of behavioral therapy that focuses on changing negative thought patterns and behaviors. In the context of autism, CBT can be used to help individuals with autism improve their perspective taking by teaching them to identify and change negative thought patterns and behaviors that are preventing them from considering the perspectives of others.

Behavioral Interventions for Improving Mind-Blindness:

Incidental Teaching: Incidental teaching is a type of behavioral intervention that involves teaching new skills in the context of natural, everyday activities. In the context of improving mind-blindness, incidental teaching can be used to teach individuals with autism about the thoughts, feelings, and beliefs of others by teaching them in the context of real-life social situations.

Reinforcement: Reinforcement is a type of behavioral intervention that involves using rewards to reinforce desired behaviors. In the context of improving mind-blindness, reinforcement can be used to reinforce behaviors such as considering the perspectives of others and understanding the thoughts, feelings, and beliefs of others.

Modeling: Modeling is a type of behavioral intervention that involves demonstrating the desired behavior for the individual with autism to observe and imitate. In the context of improving mind-blindness, modeling can be used to teach individuals with autism about the thoughts, feelings, and beliefs of others by demonstrating these behaviors for them to observe and imitate.

Conclusion: In conclusion, behavioral interventions can be effective in improving perspective taking and mind-blindness in individuals with autism. These interventions are based on the principles of behaviorism and involve teaching new skills and reinforcing desired behaviors. It is important to note that the best approach will depend on the individual and their specific needs and abilities. It is recommended that individuals with autism work with a team of professionals, including psychologists, speech therapists, and occupational therapists, to determine the best approach for their needs. Additionally, it is important to be patient and persistent in implementing these interventions, as behavior change can take time and consistent effort.

Cognitive Interventions for Perspective Taking and Mind-Blindness in Autism Spectrum Disorders

Autism Spectrum Disorders (ASD) are developmental disorders characterized by difficulties in social interaction, communication, and repetitive behaviors. One of the core features of autism is mind-blindness, or the difficulty in understanding others' thoughts, feelings, and beliefs. This difficulty in perspective taking can result in significant challenges in social interactions, relationships, and communication. In this chapter, we will focus on cognitive interventions that can be used to improve perspective taking and mind-blindness in individuals with autism.

Cognitive Interventions for Improving Perspective Taking:

Theory of Mind (ToM) Training: Theory of mind training is a type of cognitive intervention that focuses on teaching individuals with autism about the thoughts, feelings, and beliefs of others. This can involve teaching individuals about the concept of mind-reading and perspective taking, as well as practical skills for understanding and considering the perspectives of others. ToM training can be done in individual or group settings and can involve interactive activities such as role-playing and video modeling.

Cognitive Behavioral Therapy (CBT): CBT is a type of cognitive-behavioral intervention that focuses on changing negative thought patterns and behaviors. In the context of autism, CBT can be used to help individuals with autism improve their perspective taking by teaching them to identify and change negative thought patterns and behaviors that are preventing them from considering the perspectives of others.

Social Cognition Training: Social cognition training is a type of cognitive intervention that focuses on improving an individual's understanding of social information, including nonverbal cues and the thoughts, feelings, and beliefs of others. Social cognition training can involve teaching individuals about the social cues and perspectives of others, as well as practicing these skills in real-life social situations.

Cognitive Interventions for Improving Mind-Blindness:

Executive Functioning (EF) Training:

Executive functioning (EF) training is a type of cognitive intervention that focuses on improving an individual's ability to plan, organize, and complete tasks. In the context of autism and mind-blindness, EF training can be used to improve an individual's ability to understand the perspectives of others by teaching them skills for planning, organizing, and completing social tasks.

Mindfulness Training: Mindfulness training is a type of cognitive intervention that involves teaching individuals to be present and aware in the moment. In the context of autism and mind-blindness, mindfulness training can be used to improve an individual's ability to understand the perspectives of others by helping them to be more present and aware in social situations.

Cognitive Remediation Therapy (CRT): Cognitive remediation therapy is a type of cognitive intervention that focuses on improving cognitive abilities, including attention, memory, and problem-solving. In the context of autism and mind-blindness, CRT can be used to improve an individual's ability to understand the perspectives of others by improving their overall cognitive abilities.

Conclusion: In conclusion, cognitive interventions can be effective in improving perspective taking and mind-blindness in individuals with autism. These interventions are based on the principles of cognitive psychology and involve teaching new skills and changing negative thought patterns. It is important to note that the best approach will depend on the individual and their specific needs and abilities. It is recommended that individuals with autism work with a team of professionals, including psychologists, speech therapists, and occupational therapists, to determine the best approach for their needs. Additionally, it is important to be patient and persistent in implementing these interventions, as behavior change can take time and consistent effort.

Social Skills Training for Individuals with Autism Spectrum Disorders

Autism Spectrum Disorders (ASD) are developmental disorders characterized by difficulties in social interaction, communication, and repetitive behaviors. Social skills training is a type of intervention that focuses on improving the social skills of individuals with autism. This type of intervention is designed to help individuals with autism develop the skills they need to participate in social situations, form relationships, and effectively communicate with others.

Types of Social Skills Training:

Modeling: Modeling is a type of social skills training that involves demonstrating appropriate social behaviors for individuals with autism to observe and imitate. This type of training can involve watching videos of social interactions or participating in live role-playing scenarios.

Role-Playing: Role-playing is a type of social skills training that involves practicing social behaviors in a simulated environment. This type of training can involve acting out different social scenarios and receiving feedback from a therapist or instructor.

Group Social Skills Training: Group social skills training is a type of intervention that involves practicing social skills in a group setting. This type of training can involve participating in group activities, games, and discussions with other individuals with autism.

Naturalistic Teaching: Naturalistic teaching

is a type of social skills training that involves incorporating social skills training into natural, everyday activities. This type of training can involve practicing social skills in real-life social situations, such as going to a restaurant or attending a party.

Benefits of Social Skills Training:

Improved Communication: Social skills training can help individuals with autism improve their communication skills, including their ability to express themselves, understand others, and engage in conversation.

Increased Confidence: Social skills training can help individuals with autism develop confidence in their social abilities, which can improve their self-esteem and overall quality of life.

Improved Relationships: Social skills training can help individuals with autism form and maintain positive relationships with others.

This can include improving relationships with family members, friends, and romantic partners.

Enhanced Employment Opportunities: Social skills training can help individuals with autism develop the skills they need to succeed in the workplace, including communication, teamwork, and problem-solving skills.

Considerations for Social Skills Training:

Individualized Approach: It is important to tailor social skills training to the individual's specific needs and abilities. A personalized approach will ensure that the training is relevant and effective.

Age Appropriate: Social skills training should be age-appropriate, taking into consideration the developmental stage and needs of the individual.

Consistency: Consistent and regular

participation in social skills training is key to its success. Regular practice of the skills learned in social skills training is essential for their acquisition and maintenance.

Integration into Daily Life: Social skills training should be integrated into daily life as much as possible to ensure that the skills are being practiced in real-life situations.

Conclusion: In conclusion, social skills training is a valuable intervention for individuals with autism. This type of intervention can help individuals with autism develop the skills they need to participate in social situations, form relationships, and effectively communicate with others. It is important to work with a team of professionals, including psychologists, speech therapists, and occupational therapists, to determine the best approach for an individual's needs. With consistency and persistence, individuals with autism can make significant improvements in their social skills and overall quality of life.

Parent-Mediated Interventions for Autism Spectrum Disorders

Autism Spectrum Disorders (ASD) are developmental disorders characterized by difficulties in social interaction, communication, and repetitive behaviors. Parent-mediated interventions are a type of treatment that involve parents in the therapeutic process, working with their child with autism to improve social and communication skills.

Types of Parent-Mediated Interventions:

Pivotal Response Treatment (PRT): PRT is a type of parent-mediated intervention that focuses on addressing key behaviors in individuals with autism, such as communication and social interaction, to improve overall functioning. This type of intervention involves parents working with their child on specific tasks and activities to improve their skills.

Early Start Denver Model (ESDM): ESDM is a type of parent-mediated intervention that focuses on providing early and intensive therapy for children with autism. This type of intervention involves parents working with their child and a trained therapist to develop social, communication, and play skills.

Incidental Teaching: Incidental teaching is a type of parent-mediated intervention that involves incorporating social and communication skills training into natural, everyday activities. This type of intervention involves parents working with their child during everyday routines, such as mealtime or playtime, to improve their social and communication skills.

Benefits of Parent-Mediated Interventions:

Increased Family Involvement: Parent-mediated interventions allow for increased involvement and engagement of the family in the therapeutic process. This can lead to a stronger sense of connection and a deeper understanding of the child's needs and abilities.

Improved Skills Generalization: By incorporating parent-mediated interventions into the child's everyday life, the skills they learn are more likely to transfer to real-life situations. This can lead to improved overall functioning and increased independence.

Increased Access to Services: Parent-mediated interventions are often more accessible than traditional therapies, as they can be done in the home or in other community settings. This can lead to increased access to services for families who may have limited resources or transportation.

Cost-Effective: Parent-mediated interventions can be more cost-effective than traditional therapies, as they typically involve fewer resources and lower costs for trained professionals.

Considerations for Parent-Mediated Interventions:

Professional Guidance: It is important for parents to receive guidance from trained professionals, such as psychologists or therapists, to ensure that the intervention is being implemented correctly and effectively.

Consistency: Consistent and regular participation in parent-mediated interventions is key to their success. Regular practice of the skills learned in the interventions is essential for their acquisition and maintenance.

Parental Training: Parents should receive training on the specific intervention they will be implementing, as well as ongoing support and guidance as needed.

Tailored Approach: Parent-mediated interventions should be tailored to the individual needs and abilities of the child with autism. A personalized approach will ensure that the intervention is relevant and effective.

Conclusion: In conclusion, parent-mediated interventions are a valuable treatment option for individuals with autism. This type of intervention allows for increased family involvement, improved skills generalization, increased access to services, and cost-effectiveness. With professional guidance and parental training, individuals with autism and their families can make significant improvements in their social and communication skills and overall functioning.

7 ROLE OF TECHNOLOGY IN IMPROVING PERSPECTIVE TAKING AND MIND BLINDNESS IN AUTISM SPECTRUM DISORDERS

Technology and Autism Spectrum Disorder

Autism Spectrum Disorder (ASD) is a complex developmental disorder that affects social interaction, communication, and behavior. Technology has emerged as a valuable tool in helping individuals with autism to develop and improve their skills in these areas. This chapter will provide an overview of the use of technology in the treatment of autism.

Types of Technology Used in Autism Intervention:

Assistive Technology: Assistive technology refers to devices and tools that are designed to help individuals with disabilities perform everyday tasks more easily. For individuals with autism, assistive technology can help with communication, organization, and other daily living skills. Examples of assistive technology for autism include communication devices, such as augmentative and alternative communication (AAC) devices, and organizational tools, such as calendars and task lists.

Virtual Reality Technology: Virtual reality technology has become increasingly popular in the treatment of autism. This type of technology allows individuals to experience realistic simulations in a controlled environment, helping them to develop skills in areas such as social interaction and communication. Virtual reality technology can also be used to desensitize individuals with autism to potentially stressful situations, such as crowded public places.

Gaming Technology: Gaming technology is another type of technology that is often used in the treatment of autism. Gaming technology can provide individuals with autism with opportunities to practice social and communication skills in a fun and engaging way. Games can also be used to help individuals with autism develop problem-solving skills and improve attention and focus.

Benefits of Technology in Autism Intervention:

Increased Access to Services: Technology has made it possible for individuals with autism to receive services and treatment from the comfort of their own homes, increasing access to services for those who may have limited resources or transportation.

Customized Approach: Technology allows for a customized approach to treatment, tailored to the individual needs and abilities of the individual with autism. This can lead to increased effectiveness of the intervention.

Improved Skills Generalization: By incorporating technology into the treatment of autism, individuals have the opportunity to practice skills in a variety of settings, helping to improve the generalization of skills to real-life situations.

Increased Engagement: Technology can be an engaging and enjoyable way for individuals with autism to practice and develop skills. This can lead to increased motivation and participation in treatment.

Considerations for the Use of Technology

in Autism Intervention:

Professional Guidance: It is important for individuals with autism and their families to receive guidance from trained professionals, such as psychologists or therapists, to ensure that technology is being used correctly and effectively.

Age Appropriate: Technology should be age-appropriate, taking into consideration the individual's developmental stage and abilities.

Accessibility: Technology should be accessible and usable by individuals with autism, taking into consideration any physical or cognitive limitations they may have.

Evidence-Based: Technology should be evidence-based, with research demonstrating its effectiveness in the treatment of autism.

Conclusion: In conclusion, technology has emerged as a valuable tool in the treatment of autism. With assistive technology, virtual reality technology, and gaming technology, individuals with autism can improve their skills in areas such as communication, social interaction, and daily living skills. However, it is important to use technology with professional guidance, ensuring that it is age-appropriate, accessible, and evidence-based. When used effectively, technology can be a valuable tool in the treatment of autism, leading to improved skills and increased independence for individuals with autism.

Virtual Reality for Improving Perspective Taking in Autism Spectrum Disorders

Virtual reality (VR) is a technology that provides individuals with a simulated experience of a real-life situation. In recent

years, VR has emerged as a promising tool
for improving perspective taking in
individuals with autism spectrum disorders
(ASD). Perspective taking refers to the
ability to understand and consider others'
thoughts, feelings, and experiences, and is
an important aspect of social cognition.

How Virtual Reality Works for Improving Perspective Taking:

Realistic Simulations: VR allows individuals
to experience realistic simulations of social
situations, allowing them to practice
perspective taking in a controlled and safe
environment. This can help to build
confidence and improve the generalization
of skills to real-life situations.

Practice of Social Skills: VR allows
individuals to practice social skills, such as
initiating conversations, understanding
body language, and interpreting emotional
expressions. This can help to improve the

individual's ability to take the perspective of others.

Desensitization: VR can also be used to desensitize individuals with ASD to potentially stressful situations, such as crowded public places, helping them to develop resilience and improve perspective taking.

Benefits of Virtual Reality for Improving Perspective Taking:

Increased Engagement: VR can be an engaging and enjoyable way for individuals with ASD to practice and develop perspective taking skills. This can lead to increased motivation and participation in treatment.

Improved Generalization of Skills: By incorporating VR into the treatment of ASD, individuals have the opportunity to practice perspective taking skills in a variety of realistic and challenging situations, helping to improve the generalization of skills to real-life situations.

Customized Approach: VR allows for a customized approach to treatment, tailored to the individual needs and abilities of the individual with ASD. This can lead to increased effectiveness of the intervention.

Considerations for the Use of Virtual Reality in Improving Perspective Taking:

Professional Guidance: It is important for individuals with ASD and their families to receive guidance from trained professionals, such as psychologists or therapists, to ensure that VR is being used correctly and effectively.

Age Appropriate: VR should be age-appropriate, taking into consideration the individual's developmental stage and abilities.

Accessibility: VR should be accessible and

usable by individuals with ASD, taking into consideration any physical or cognitive limitations they may have.

Evidence-Based: VR should be evidence-based, with research demonstrating its effectiveness in improving perspective taking in individuals with ASD.

Conclusion: In conclusion, VR has emerged as a promising tool for improving perspective taking in individuals with ASD. By providing realistic simulations of social situations and allowing individuals to practice social skills, VR can help to build confidence and improve the generalization of skills to real-life situations. However, it is important to use VR with professional guidance, ensuring that it is age-appropriate, accessible, and evidence-based. When used effectively, VR can be a valuable tool in the treatment of ASD, leading to improved perspective taking skills and increased social interaction for individuals with ASD.

Robotics for Improving Mind-Blindness in Autism Spectrum Disorders

Robotics is an area of technology that involves the design, construction, and use of robots. In recent years, robotics has emerged as a promising tool for improving mind-blindness in individuals with autism spectrum disorders (ASD). Mind-blindness refers to the difficulty in understanding and considering others' thoughts, feelings, and experiences, and is a core aspect of the social cognition difficulties seen in individuals with ASD.

How Robotics Works for Improving Mind-Blindness:

Social Interaction: Robotics can provide individuals with ASD an opportunity to practice social interaction and perspective taking skills in a controlled and safe environment. This can help to build confidence and improve the individual's ability to take the perspective of others.

Practice of Social Skills: Robotics can also be used to help individuals with ASD practice specific social skills, such as initiating conversations, understanding body language, and interpreting emotional expressions. This can lead to improved mind-blindness.

Customized Approach: Robotics can be customized to meet the individual needs and abilities of individuals with ASD, allowing for a tailored approach to treatment.

Benefits of Robotics for Improving Mind-Blindness:

Increased Engagement: Robotics can be an engaging and enjoyable way for individuals with ASD to practice and develop mind-blindness skills. This can lead to increased motivation and participation in treatment.

Improved Generalization of Skills: By incorporating robotics into the treatment of ASD, individuals have the opportunity to practice mind-blindness skills in a variety of realistic and challenging situations, helping to improve the generalization of skills to real-life situations.

Increased Understanding: Robotics can provide individuals with ASD with a visual and interactive representation of the mental states and experiences of others, helping to increase their understanding and consideration of others.

Considerations for the Use of Robotics in Improving Mind-Blindness:

Professional Guidance: It is important for individuals with ASD and their families to receive guidance from trained professionals, such as psychologists or therapists, to ensure that robotics is being used correctly and effectively.

Age Appropriate: Robotics should be age-appropriate, taking into consideration the individual's developmental stage and abilities.

Accessibility: Robotics should be accessible and usable by individuals with ASD, taking into consideration any physical or cognitive limitations they may have.

Evidence-Based: Robotics should be evidence-based, with research demonstrating its effectiveness in improving mind-blindness in individuals with ASD.

Conclusion: In conclusion, robotics has emerged as a promising tool for improving mind-blindness in individuals with ASD. By providing an opportunity to practice social interaction and specific social skills in a controlled and safe environment, robotics can help to build confidence and improve the individual's ability to take the perspective of others. However, it is important to use robotics with professional guidance, ensuring that it is age-appropriate, accessible, and evidence-based. When used effectively, robotics can be a valuable tool in the treatment of ASD, leading to improved mind-blindness and increased social interaction for individuals with ASD.

Augmented Reality for Improving Social Skills in Autism Spectrum Disorders

Augmented Reality (AR) is a technology that combines the real world with virtual elements to create a blended environment. AR has been used in various fields, including education and health, and is increasingly being explored as a tool for improving social skills in individuals with autism spectrum disorders (ASD).

How Augmented Reality Works for Improving Social Skills:

Simulation of Real-Life Situations: AR can simulate real-life social situations, allowing individuals with ASD to practice social skills in a controlled and safe environment. This can help to build confidence and improve the individual's ability to respond appropriately to social situations.

Practice of Social Cues: AR can also be used to help individuals with ASD practice identifying and responding to social cues, such as body language, emotional expressions, and tone of voice. This can lead to improved social skills.

Customized Approach: AR can be customized to meet the individual needs and abilities of individuals with ASD, allowing for a tailored approach to treatment.

Benefits of Augmented Reality for Improving Social Skills:

Increased Engagement: AR can be an engaging and enjoyable way for individuals with ASD to practice and develop social skills. This can lead to increased motivation and participation in treatment.

Improved Generalization of Skills: By incorporating AR into the treatment of ASD, individuals have the opportunity to practice social skills in a variety of realistic and challenging situations, helping to improve the generalization of skills to real-life situations.

Increased Awareness: AR can provide individuals with ASD with a visual and interactive representation of the social cues and experiences of others, helping to increase their awareness and understanding of social situations.

Considerations for the Use of Augmented

Reality in Improving Social Skills:

Professional Guidance: It is important for individuals with ASD and their families to receive guidance from trained professionals, such as psychologists or therapists, to ensure that AR is being used correctly and effectively.

Age Appropriate: AR should be age-appropriate, taking into consideration the individual's developmental stage and abilities.

Accessibility: AR should be accessible and usable by individuals with ASD, taking into consideration any physical or cognitive limitations they may have.

Evidence-Based: AR should be evidence-based, with research demonstrating its effectiveness in improving social skills in individuals with ASD.

Conclusion: In conclusion, AR is a promising

tool for improving social skills in individuals with ASD. By providing an opportunity to practice social interaction and social cues in a controlled and safe environment, AR can help to build confidence and improve the individual's ability to respond appropriately to social situations. However, it is important to use AR with professional guidance, ensuring that it is age-appropriate, accessible, and evidence-based. When used effectively, AR can be a valuable tool in the treatment of ASD, leading to improved social skills and increased social interaction for individuals with ASD.

8 SUPPORTING INDIVIDUALS WITH AUTISM SPECTRUM DISORDER IN EVERYDAY LIFE

Supporting Individuals with Autism Spectrum Disorder in Everyday Life

Autism Spectrum Disorder (ASD) is a complex developmental disorder that affects social interaction, communication, and behavior. Supporting individuals with ASD in everyday life can be challenging, but it can also be incredibly rewarding. In this chapter, we will explore strategies for supporting individuals with ASD in various aspects of their lives, including communication, social interaction, education, and employment.

Communication:

Speech and Language Therapy: Individuals with ASD may have difficulty with communication and language. Speech and language therapy can help improve communication skills and develop new language skills.

Augmentative and Alternative Communication (AAC): For individuals with severe communication difficulties, AAC may be necessary. This may include sign language, communication boards, and voice output devices.

Visual Supports: Visual aids such as pictures, schedules, and social stories can help individuals with ASD understand expectations and routines.

Social Interaction:

Social Skills Training: Social skills training can help individuals with ASD develop their understanding of social cues and improve their ability to interact with others.

Group Activities: Participating in group activities, such as sports or music groups, can provide opportunities for individuals with ASD to interact with peers and build relationships.

Role-Play: Role-playing social scenarios can help individuals with ASD practice their social skills in a controlled and safe environment.

Education:

Individualized Education Plan (IEP): An IEP is a tailored education plan that takes into consideration the individual needs of the student with ASD.

Inclusive Education: Inclusive education means that students with ASD are placed in a regular classroom alongside their peers. This can provide opportunities for social interaction and peer modeling.

Accommodations: Accommodations, such as extra time on tests, a quiet workspace, or visual aids, can help individuals with ASD be successful in their education.

Employment:

Supported Employment: Supported employment involves assistance in finding and maintaining employment. This can include job coaching and ongoing support.

Job Accommodations: Job accommodations, such as a modified work schedule or a quiet workspace, can help individuals with ASD be successful in their employment.

Entrepreneurship: Entrepreneurship can provide individuals with ASD with the opportunity to use their skills and interests in a self-employed capacity.

Conclusion: In conclusion, supporting individuals with ASD in everyday life requires a personalized approach that takes into consideration the individual needs and abilities of the individual. Communication, social interaction, education, and employment are all areas where support can make a significant impact on the quality of life for individuals with ASD. It is important to work with professionals, such as educators, therapists, and employment specialists, to develop a comprehensive support plan that addresses the unique needs of the individual with ASD. With the right support and accommodations,

individuals with ASD can lead fulfilling and
successful lives.

Strategies for Supporting Individuals with Autism Spectrum Disorders in the Workplace

Autism Spectrum Disorder (ASD) is a
neurodevelopmental disorder that affects
social interaction, communication, and
behavior. Despite the challenges posed by
ASD, many individuals with the disorder are
capable of working and contributing to
society. However, it can be challenging for
individuals with ASD to find and maintain
employment. In this chapter, we will
explore strategies for supporting individuals
with ASD in the workplace.

Job Accommodations: Job
accommodations, such as a modified work
schedule, a quiet workspace, or visual aids,
can help individuals with ASD be successful

in their employment.

Job Coaching: Job coaching can provide support and guidance to individuals with ASD as they navigate the workplace. This can include assistance with job tasks, social interactions, and communication.

Sensory Accommodations: For individuals with sensory sensitivities, sensory accommodations, such as reducing noise levels or providing a quiet space, can help create a comfortable work environment.

Social Skills Training: Social skills training can help individuals with ASD improve their understanding of social cues and improve their ability to interact with others in the workplace.

Clear Expectations and Rules: Clearly communicated expectations and rules can help individuals with ASD understand what is expected of them in the workplace.

Flexibility: Allowing for flexibility in the workplace, such as adjusting work hours or providing breaks, can help individuals with ASD manage their work-related stress.

Awareness and Acceptance: Creating a workplace culture of awareness and acceptance can help individuals with ASD feel valued and supported. This can include providing training and education to co-workers on autism and its effects.

Collaboration: Collaborating with professionals, such as job coaches, speech therapists, and occupational therapists, can help support individuals with ASD in the workplace and ensure their success.

Conclusion: In conclusion, supporting individuals with ASD in the workplace requires a collaborative and individualized approach. Accommodations, job coaching, social skills training, and a workplace culture of awareness and acceptance can all play a role in supporting individuals with ASD in the workplace. It is important for employers and co-workers to understand the unique needs of individuals with ASD and work together to create a supportive work environment that allows for success and fulfillment. By providing the right support and accommodations, individuals with ASD can thrive in the workplace and make valuable contributions to society.

Supporting Individuals with Autism Spectrum Disorders in Education

Autism Spectrum Disorder (ASD) is a neurodevelopmental disorder that affects social interaction, communication, and behavior. Many individuals with ASD are capable of pursuing an education and reaching their full potential with the right support. In this chapter, we will explore strategies for supporting individuals with

ASD in education.

Individualized Education Plans (IEPs): An
Individualized Education Plan (IEP) is a legal
document that outlines the specific support
and accommodations a student with
disabilities needs to succeed in the
classroom. An IEP can include modifications
to the classroom environment, teaching
strategies, and assessments.

Classroom Accommodations: Classroom
accommodations, such as a quiet
workspace or visual aids, can help
individuals with ASD be successful in their
education.

Social Skills Training: Social skills training
can help individuals with ASD improve their
understanding of social cues and improve
their ability to interact with others in the
classroom.

Collaboration with Specialists: Collaborating
with specialists, such as speech therapists,

occupational therapists, and psychologists, can help support individuals with ASD in the classroom and ensure their success.

Technology: Technology, such as assistive technology, can help individuals with ASD access and participate in the curriculum.

Positive Behavior Support: Positive behavior support involves reinforcing positive behavior and providing consequences for inappropriate behavior. This approach can help individuals with ASD manage their behavior in the classroom.

Flexibility: Allowing for flexibility in the classroom, such as adjusting the pace of instruction or providing breaks, can help individuals with ASD manage their stress and be successful in their education.

Teacher Training: Providing training and education to teachers on autism and its effects can help create a supportive and inclusive classroom environment for individuals with ASD.

Conclusion: In conclusion, supporting individuals with ASD in education requires a collaborative and individualized approach. Individualized Education Plans, classroom accommodations, social skills training, and positive behavior support can all play a role in supporting individuals with ASD in the education setting. It is important for educators and school administrators to understand the unique needs of individuals with ASD and work together to create a supportive learning environment that allows for success and fulfillment. By providing the right support and accommodations, individuals with ASD can thrive in their education and reach their full potential.

Supporting Individuals with Autism Spectrum Disorders in Social Settings

Autism Spectrum Disorder (ASD) affects individuals' ability to engage in social interaction and understand social cues, making social settings challenging for many individuals with ASD. In this chapter, we will explore strategies for supporting individuals with ASD in social settings.

Social Stories: Social stories are narratives that provide a visual and written explanation of a social situation, including expected behavior and social cues. They can help individuals with ASD understand and prepare for social situations.

Visual Supports: Visual supports, such as schedules, maps, and visual cues, can help individuals with ASD understand and navigate social situations.

Social Skills Training: Social skills training can help individuals with ASD improve their understanding of social cues and improve their ability to interact with others in social situations.

Practice: Providing opportunities for individuals with ASD to practice their social skills in structured and supportive settings can help build their confidence and prepare them for real-life social situations.

Communication Supports: Communication supports, such as picture exchange communication systems, can help individuals with ASD communicate their wants and needs in social situations.

Collaboration with Support Network: Collaborating with individuals' support network, such as parents, caregivers, and other professionals, can help ensure that individuals with ASD have the support they need in social situations.

Flexibility: Allowing for flexibility in social situations, such as adjusting the pace or activities, can help individuals with ASD manage their stress and be successful in social settings.

Peer Support: Peer support, such as peer mentoring and social groups, can provide individuals with ASD with the opportunity to practice their social skills and build relationships with their peers.

Conclusion: In conclusion, supporting individuals with ASD in social settings requires a comprehensive and individualized approach. Social stories, visual supports, social skills training, and communication supports can all play a role in supporting individuals with ASD in social situations. It is important for individuals' support network to understand the unique needs of individuals with ASD and work together to create a supportive social environment that allows for success and fulfillment. By providing the right support and accommodations, individuals with ASD can navigate and thrive in social situations.

9 ADVOCATING FOR INDIVIDUALS WITH AUTISM SPECTRUM DISORDER

Advocating for Individuals with Autism Spectrum Disorders

Advocacy is an important part of ensuring that individuals with Autism Spectrum Disorders (ASD) receive the support and resources they need. This chapter will explore strategies for advocating for individuals with ASD.

Understanding the Law: Familiarizing yourself with laws, such as the Individuals with Disabilities Education Act (IDEA) and

the Americans with Disabilities Act (ADA),
can help ensure that individuals with ASD
receive the support and accommodations
they need.

Building a Support Network: Building a
network of advocates, including parents,
caregivers, professionals, and other
individuals with ASD, can help increase your
impact as an advocate.

Staying Informed: Keeping up-to-date with
current research, resources, and news
related to ASD can help you be a well-
informed advocate.

Connecting with Local Resources:
Connecting with local organizations and
resources, such as support groups and
advocacy organizations, can help you stay
informed and connected to the community.

Building Relationships: Building
relationships with individuals and
organizations that can support your

advocacy efforts, such as schools, healthcare providers, and government agencies, can help increase your impact as an advocate.

Speaking Up: Speaking up and sharing your experiences as an individual with ASD or as a caregiver of someone with ASD can raise awareness and create change.

Creating Awareness: Participating in events, such as Autism Awareness Month, and sharing information about ASD with others can help raise awareness and create change.

Participating in the Political Process: Participating in the political process, such as writing letters to elected officials and attending town hall meetings, can help ensure that the needs of individuals with ASD are heard and addressed.

Conclusion: In conclusion, advocating for individuals with ASD requires a comprehensive and persistent approach. Understanding the law, building a support network, staying informed, and connecting with local resources can all play a role in effective advocacy. Building relationships, speaking up, creating awareness, and participating in the political process can also help make a difference in the lives of individuals with ASD. By advocating for individuals with ASD, we can create a more inclusive and supportive community for everyone.

Understanding the Legal Rights of Individuals with Autism Spectrum Disorders

Individuals with Autism Spectrum Disorders (ASD) have legal rights that protect them from discrimination and ensure they receive appropriate support and services. This chapter will provide an overview of the legal rights of individuals with ASD.

The Americans with Disabilities Act (ADA):
The ADA is a federal law that prohibits
discrimination against individuals with
disabilities in employment, housing, and
other areas.

The Individuals with Disabilities Education
Act (IDEA): IDEA is a federal law that
guarantees a free and appropriate
education to children with disabilities,
including those with ASD.

The Fair Housing Act (FHA): The FHA is a
federal law that prohibits discrimination in
housing based on disability.

Section 504 of the Rehabilitation Act:
Section 504 is a federal law that prohibits
discrimination against individuals with
disabilities in programs and activities that
receive federal financial assistance.

State and Local Laws: In addition to federal

laws, some states and localities have laws that provide additional protections for individuals with disabilities, including those with ASD.

Legal Advocacy: Legal advocacy is the process of advocating for the legal rights of individuals with disabilities, including those with ASD. Legal advocates can provide information, guidance, and representation to individuals with ASD and their families.

The Right to Receive Appropriate Services: Individuals with ASD have the right to receive appropriate services and support, including special education services, behavioral health services, and support in daily living activities.

The Right to Participate in Community Activities: Individuals with ASD have the right to participate in community activities, such as recreational programs, community events, and social groups.

The Right to Receive Accommodations: Individuals with ASD have the right to receive reasonable accommodations in the workplace, in housing, and in other areas to ensure they have equal access and opportunity.

Conclusion: In conclusion, individuals with ASD have legal rights that protect them from discrimination and ensure they receive appropriate support and services. Understanding these rights, connecting with legal advocates, and participating in advocacy efforts can help individuals with ASD and their families navigate the legal system and secure the support they need. By understanding the legal rights of individuals with ASD, we can create a more inclusive and supportive community for everyone.

Navigating the Healthcare System for

Individuals with Autism Spectrum Disorders

Introduction

Navigating the healthcare system can be a complex and overwhelming experience for individuals with autism spectrum disorders (ASD) and their families. This chapter will provide a comprehensive overview of the various healthcare services that individuals with ASD may need and how to access these services effectively. The goal is to help families understand their rights and responsibilities and to empower them to advocate for their loved ones.

Understanding the Healthcare System

The healthcare system is complex, with a wide range of services and providers. It is important to understand the different types of services available and the role of each provider in order to access the right care at the right time.

Primary Care Providers (PCPs)

Primary care providers (PCPs) are usually the first point of contact for individuals with ASD when seeking medical care. They provide general medical care, including routine check-ups, vaccinations, and treatment for minor illnesses and injuries. PCPs can also help diagnose and manage medical conditions and refer patients to specialists when necessary.

Specialists

Specialists are medical professionals with expertise in a specific area of medicine, such as neurology, psychiatry, or speech and language therapy. They provide specialized care for individuals with ASD and can help manage complex medical conditions, such as seizure disorders, sleep disorders, and behavioral problems.

Therapies

Therapies, such as speech and language therapy, occupational therapy, and physical therapy, are an important part of healthcare for individuals with ASD. These therapies can help improve communication, motor skills, and daily living activities.

Mental Health Services

Mental health services, such as counseling and therapy, are important for individuals with ASD who may experience anxiety, depression, or other mental health issues. These services can help individuals and their families manage the social and emotional challenges that may arise with an ASD diagnosis.

Accessing Healthcare Services

The first step in accessing healthcare services is to find a PCP who is knowledgeable about autism spectrum disorders. It is important to find a provider who is willing to work with individuals with

ASD and their families, and who is familiar with the various services and resources available.

Insurance

Health insurance is a crucial aspect of accessing healthcare services for individuals with ASD. Insurance can cover the cost of doctor visits, medications, and therapies. The type of insurance and the specific benefits it provides will vary depending on the individual's plan.

Family support

Family support is critical in navigating the healthcare system for individuals with ASD. Family members can provide emotional support and help with communication and decision-making during medical appointments. They can also serve as advocates for their loved ones and help ensure that they receive the care they need.

Advocacy and Resources

Advocacy is the act of speaking out on behalf of individuals with autism spectrum disorders and their families. There are many organizations and resources available that can help families with advocacy, such as local autism organizations, advocacy groups, and government agencies.

Conclusion

The healthcare system can be a complex and overwhelming experience for individuals with autism spectrum disorders and their families. It is important to understand the different types of services available and the role of each provider in order to access the right care at the right time. By seeking out the right healthcare services, working with insurance providers, and utilizing advocacy and support resources, individuals with autism and their families can receive the care and support they need.

Building Supportive Communities for Individuals with Autism Spectrum Disorders

Autism Spectrum Disorder (ASD) affects approximately 1 in 59 individuals globally and is a neurodevelopmental disorder characterized by impairments in social communication and interaction, as well as repetitive or restrictive behaviors. Individuals with autism can face numerous challenges in everyday life and require support from their families, friends, and communities.

In this chapter, we will discuss the importance of building supportive communities for individuals with autism and how this can greatly improve their quality of life.

The Importance of Community Support

A supportive community can provide individuals with autism the necessary resources and support to help them thrive in their personal, educational, and professional lives. This includes having access to educational and employment opportunities, healthcare services, and a safe and inclusive living environment.

Moreover, individuals with autism often face social isolation and lack of understanding from their peers. A supportive community can help break down these barriers and provide individuals with autism the opportunity to form meaningful relationships, develop their social skills, and feel a sense of belonging.

Building a Supportive Community

Education and Awareness: Education and awareness are the first steps in building a supportive community for individuals with autism. By educating the community about the characteristics and needs of individuals with autism, we can reduce stigma and increase understanding. This can be achieved through community events, workshops, and information sessions.

Inclusive Environments: Creating inclusive environments, such as schools, workplaces, and public spaces, can greatly improve the quality of life for individuals with autism. This includes ensuring access to appropriate accommodations and support services, promoting positive attitudes and behaviors, and providing training for staff and peers.

Peer-to-Peer Support: Peer-to-peer support can be a powerful tool for individuals with autism. This can involve creating opportunities for individuals with autism to connect with others who have similar experiences, such as through social skills groups or online forums.

Family and Caregiver Support: Family and caregivers play a crucial role in the lives of individuals with autism and need support as well. This can include access to resources and support services, opportunities for respite care, and support groups where they can connect with other families and caregivers.

Collaboration and Partnership: Collaborating with organizations and agencies that serve individuals with autism can help build a more supportive community. This can include partnerships with schools, healthcare providers, and local government organizations to ensure that individuals with autism receive the support and services they need.

Conclusion

Building a supportive community for individuals with autism requires a collective effort from all members of society. By promoting education and awareness, creating inclusive environments, providing peer-to-peer support, supporting families and caregivers, and collaborating with organizations and agencies, we can create a world that is more supportive and inclusive for individuals with autism.

The goal of this chapter is to raise awareness about the importance of building supportive communities for individuals with autism and to provide practical strategies for achieving this goal. It is essential that we work together to provide individuals with autism the support and resources they need to reach their full potential.

10 CONCLUSION

The concept of perspective taking and mind-blindness is a crucial aspect of understanding the social difficulties experienced by individuals with autism spectrum disorders (ASD).

Key findings in this area of research have shown that individuals with ASD have difficulties in understanding the mental states and perspectives of others, often referred to as mind-blindness. This lack of mentalizing ability is thought to contribute to the social impairments experienced by individuals with ASD, including difficulties in social communication, interactions, and relationships.

Research has also demonstrated that perspective taking and mind-blindness in individuals with ASD can be improved through targeted interventions. These interventions can include behavioral, cognitive, and social skills training, as well as parent-mediated approaches and the use of technology such as virtual reality and robotics.

Studies have also highlighted the importance of considering individual differences among individuals with ASD, as some may have better perspective taking abilities than others. Additionally, some evidence suggests that age and other factors may impact the development of perspective taking skills in individuals with

ASD.

Overall, the research on perspective taking and mind-blindness in individuals with autism spectrum disorders highlights the need for comprehensive and individualized support to help these individuals improve their social abilities and participate in society to the fullest extent possible.

Perspective Taking and Mind-Blindness in Individuals with Autism Spectrum Disorders: Implications for Future Research

Introduction: Autism Spectrum Disorders (ASD) are neurodevelopmental conditions characterized by difficulties in social interaction, communication, and repetitive behaviors. One of the most studied aspects of ASD is perspective taking, which refers to the ability to understand others' thoughts, feelings, and perspectives. Many individuals with ASD have been found to have difficulties in perspective taking and are often referred to as having "mind-blindness."

Current Research Findings: Recent studies have shown that individuals with ASD have reduced brain activity in regions associated with perspective taking, such as the medial prefrontal cortex and the temporo-parietal junction. They also have difficulties in interpreting the mental states of others and tend to rely on the literal interpretation of language, making it difficult for them to understand sarcasm or figurative language. Additionally, individuals with ASD show reduced eye contact, which has been shown to be related to their difficulties in understanding the perspectives of others.

Implications for Future Research: Future research should focus on better understanding the neural mechanisms underlying perspective taking in individuals with ASD. This can be achieved through the use of neuroimaging techniques, such as functional magnetic resonance imaging (fMRI) or magnetoencephalography (MEG), which can provide insight into the brain regions and networks involved in perspective taking in individuals with and without ASD.

Another area of focus for future research should be the development of interventions that target perspective taking in individuals with ASD. Currently, there is limited research in this area, and interventions tend to focus on improving social skills more broadly, rather than specifically targeting perspective taking.

In addition, there is a need for research that investigates the role of individual differences in perspective taking abilities in individuals with ASD. For example, some individuals with ASD may have a relatively high level of perspective taking abilities, while others may have very low levels. This variability in perspective taking abilities within the autism spectrum may impact the effectiveness of interventions and should be studied further.

Conclusion: In conclusion, perspective taking and mind-blindness in individuals with autism spectrum disorders are important areas of research, as they play a crucial role in social interaction and communication. Future research should aim to better understand the neural mechanisms underlying perspective taking in individuals with ASD and develop interventions that target this ability. Additionally, there is a need to investigate the role of individual differences in perspective taking abilities within the autism spectrum.

Conclusion: Autism Spectrum Disorders (ASD) are neurodevelopmental conditions that can impact an individual's ability to communicate, interact with others, and engage in everyday activities. The wide range of symptoms and severity levels associated with autism can make it challenging to support individuals with this condition. However, with a combination of interventions, support, and understanding, individuals with ASD can lead fulfilling and meaningful lives.

Interventions: Interventions aimed at supporting individuals with autism can vary depending on the individual's specific needs and abilities. Some common interventions include behavior and communication therapy, social skills training, and medication for co-occurring conditions. It is important to tailor interventions to the individual and their unique needs, as well as to involve the individual and their family in the decision-making process.

Community Support: Community support

plays a crucial role in helping individuals with autism lead fulfilling lives. This includes creating inclusive environments, providing access to resources, and promoting understanding and acceptance of individuals with autism. Additionally, support from friends, family, and healthcare providers can help individuals with autism to overcome challenges and reach their full potential.

Final Thoughts: Supporting individuals with autism requires a comprehensive approach that addresses the individual's unique needs and abilities. It is important to recognize that autism is a spectrum and that each individual with autism is unique. With the right interventions, support, and understanding, individuals with autism can lead fulfilling and meaningful lives. Additionally, it is crucial to continue researching and developing new approaches to support individuals with autism, as well as to raise awareness and understanding of the condition within society.

ABOUT THE AUTHOR

Author, autism expert, and trombone player from Huntington, Indiana living in Fort Wayne. Exploring the world through travel and connecting with family - especially my two nieces and my sister. Passionate about social behavior.

Seeing Through the Mind's Eye: Navigating Perspective Taking and
Mind Blindness in Autism